the teacher who lost her smile

Written by Bec Wright
Illustrated by Crystal Leonardi

GW00685559

For Daniel and Alex
Follow your dreams, however random they may be,
for I will always have your back.
Ditto xx Wuv you xx

First published in Far North Queensland, 2024 by Bowerbird Publishing

Copyright @ 2024 Bec Wright

ISBN 978-1-7635643-7-4 (paperback)
ISBN 978-1-7635643-8-1 (ebook)

The Teacher Who Lost Her Smile
Bec Wright

First edition: 2024

Illustrations by: Crystal Leonardi, Bowerbird Publishing
Edited by: Crystal Leonardi, Bowerbird Publishing
Cover & Interior Design by: Crystal Leonardi, Bowerbird Publishing

Distributed by Bowerbird Publishing
Available in National Library of Australia

Crystal Leonardi, Bowerbird Publishing
Julatten, Queensland, Australia
www.crystalleonardi.com

❤

TEACHING IS A WORK OF HEART

CERTIFICATE OF APPRECIATION

FOR YOU

_____

Dated: _____

From: _____

Once there was a teacher who lost her *smile*.

She was very **sad...**

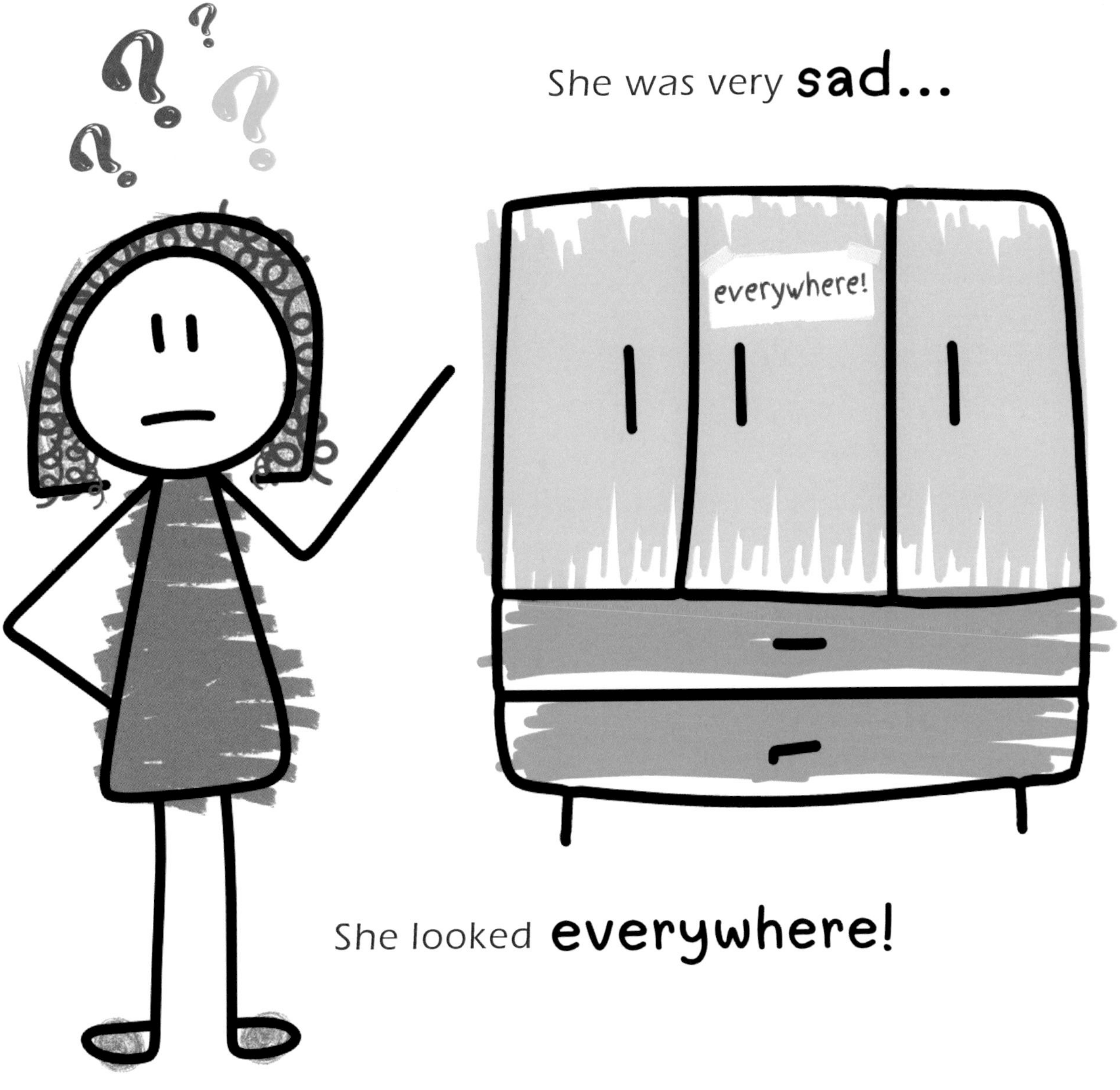
everywhere!

She looked **everywhere!**

She **thought** to herself...

Was her smile buried in the stacks of report cards she devoted her entire weekend to marking, thereby missing out on the party she desperately wanted to attend?

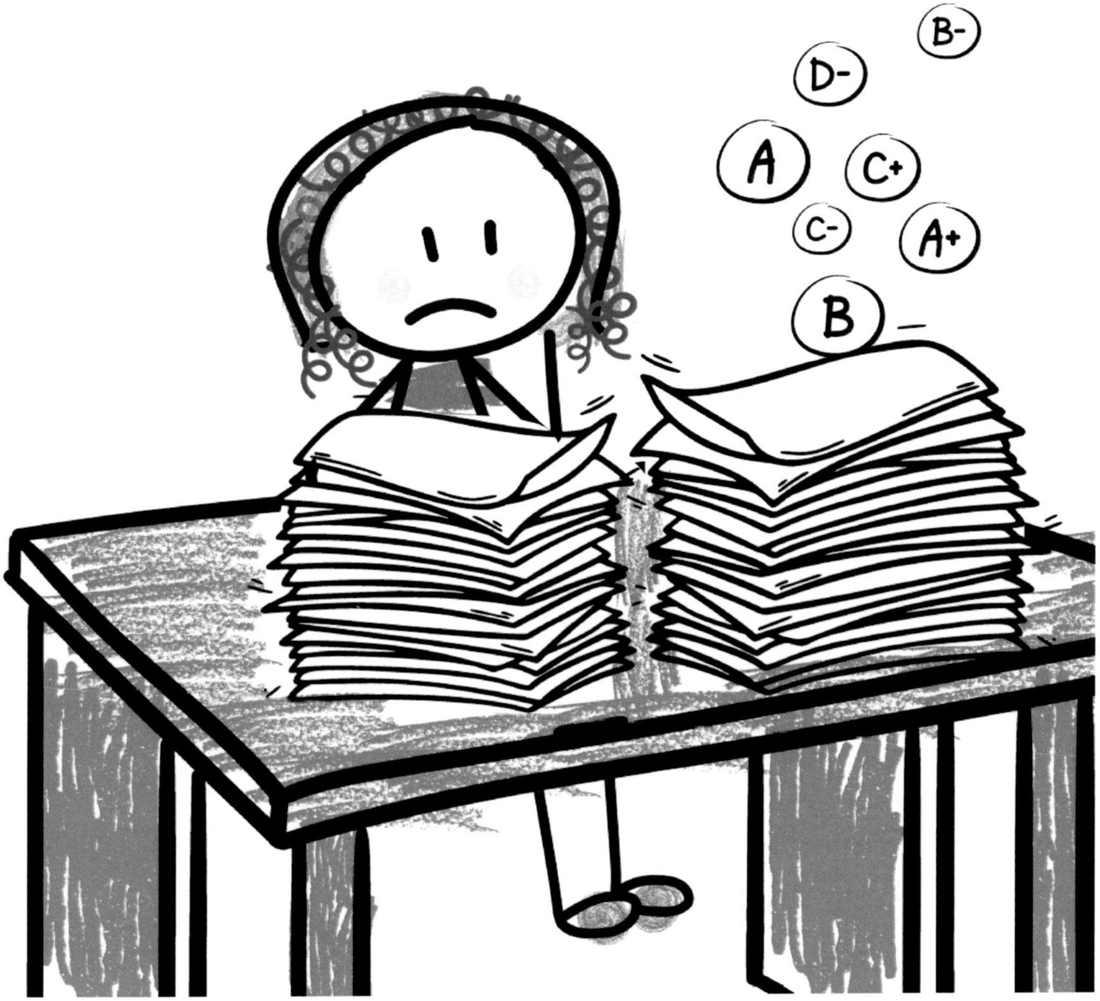
B-
D-
A
C+
C-
A+
B

Noooooo...

She **thought** to herself...

Was it lost during the staff meeting that dragged on for**EVVAARRR**, where they discussed 'what your classroom should look like' (even though she had done her degree and wondered if she didn't know by now, she shouldn't really be teaching)?

Or, could her smile have been found in the 'new' literacy strategy that admin pitched as '**ONLY** an extra 10 minutes' per day? Which added to her already full schedule of curriculum planning, music, sports, library duties, religious activities, parades, hosting special guests, concert rehearsals, grandparent visits, and jam-packed excursion days.

Noooooo...

She **thought** to herself...

Was her smile hidden in the bathroom, a place she had longed to reach all day? (even though the students had asked and been granted permission to go **49** times in the first session alone)?

... or was it on playground duty where she had reminded the students not to run on the concrete **187** times?

Nooooooo...

She **thought** to herself...

Could her smile be in the perceived '**free time**' teachers supposedly enjoy outside the hours of 9 to 3... or in the assumed 12 weeks of uninterrupted holidays that **non-teachers** believe they receive each year?

Little did they know, she had to dedicate the week prior to school for professional development and spend hours preparing for a class she wasn't certain would be hers, as it could potentially change on the notorious '**DAY 8**.'

This doesn't even account for the mental and physical planning she did during the **entire** school holidays.

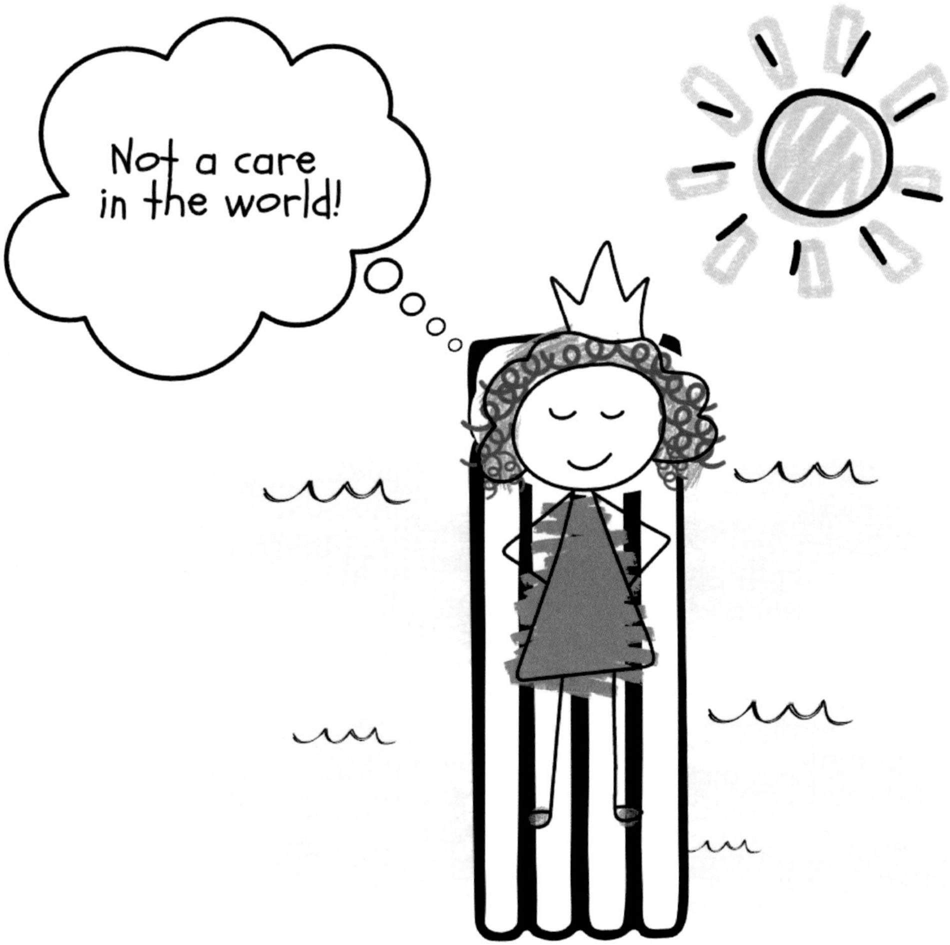
Not a care in the world!

Noooooo...

She **thought** to herself...

Was her smile tucked away in the staff room, that elusive place she never seemed to have enough time to visit because she was always occupied with marking, counselling, and listening to stories from students that seemed to stretch on endlessly?

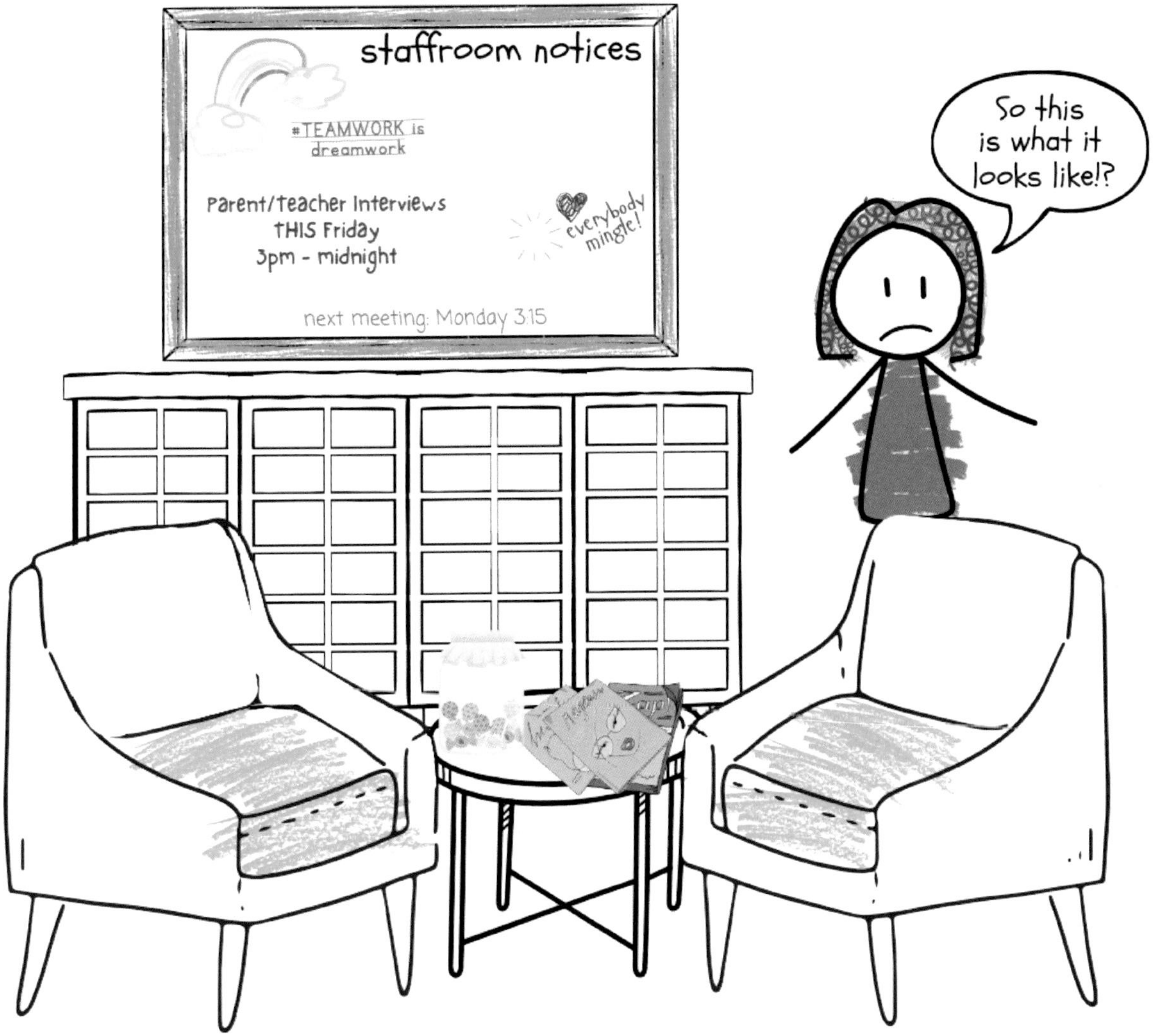
staffroom notices
#TEAMWORK is dreamwork
Parent/teacher Interviews
THIS Friday
3pm - midnight
everybody mingle!
next meeting: Monday 3:15
So this is what it looks like!?

Nooooo...

She **thought** to herself...

Was it even fathomable to consider that her smile might be found on the chair of the student she had sent to the Responsible Thinking Room, despite the fact that the student had not yet shown signs of responsible thinking?

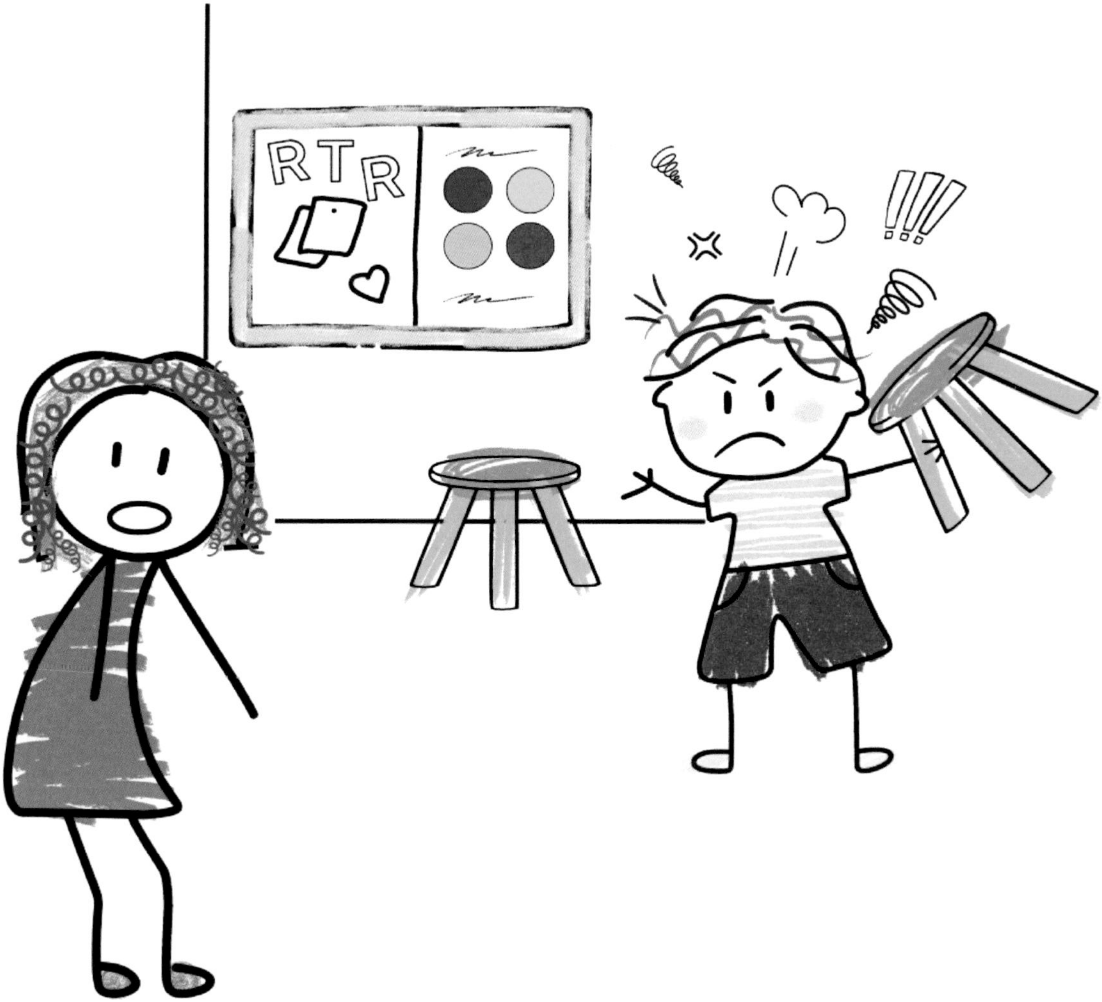
RTR

Noooooo...

She **thought** to herself...

Perhaps it lay within the pile of schoolbooks belonging to the student who was about to depart for another school in just ten minutes.

Admin had called five minutes ago, interrupting her teaching time, to alert her that the parents were on their way. She could already foresee that the child's supplies would fall short of the parent's expectations and demands.

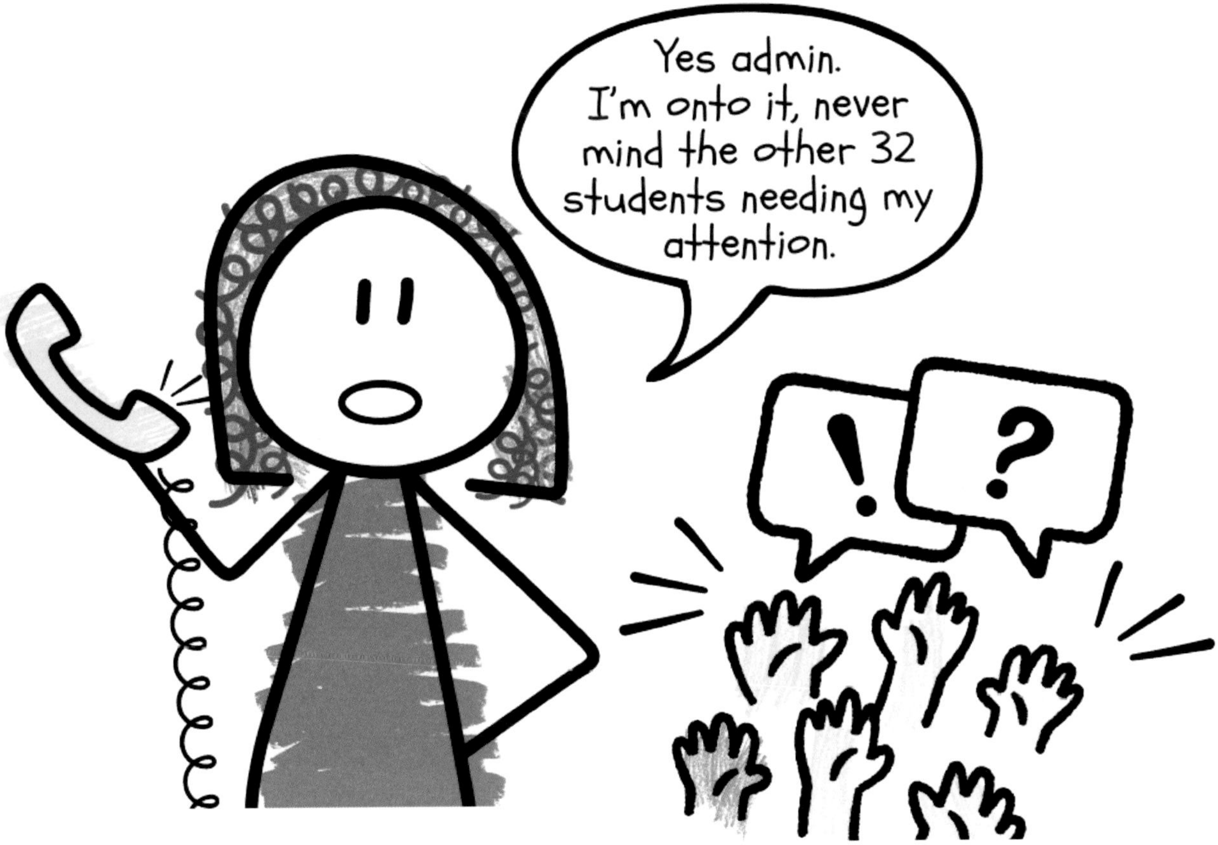
Yes admin.
I'm onto it, never mind the other 32 students needing my attention.
!
?

Noooooo...

She **thought** to herself...

Could her smile possibly be in the hundreds (or even thousands) of dollars she had invested in purchasing additional school resources?

These were the purchases her family didn't necessarily support, including spare pencils, erasers, paper, extra books, stickers, highlighters, glue, laminating sheets, and rewards for the prize box.

Or, was it among the posters, desk caddies, room decals, and curtains she had purchased to create a warm and inviting learning environment for her students?

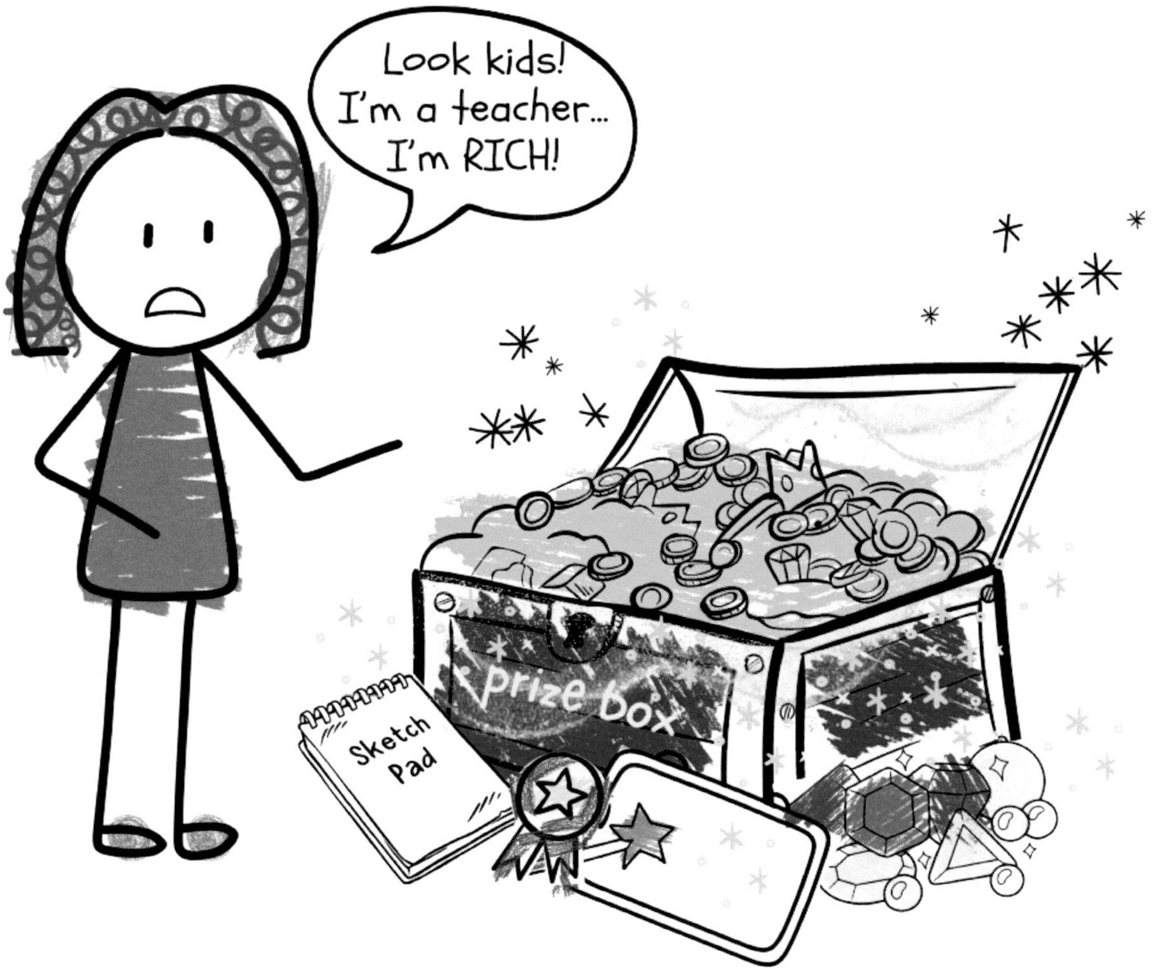
Look kids!
I'm a teacher...
I'm RICH!
prize box
Sketch Pad

Noooooo...

She **thought** to herself...

Alternatively, it might just be found in the moments it took for the children to understand that when she requested them to take out their books, she meant *now!*

Or in the time it took for them to remember where to write their name, even though she reminded them
E-v-e-r-y S-i-n-g-l-e D-a-y!

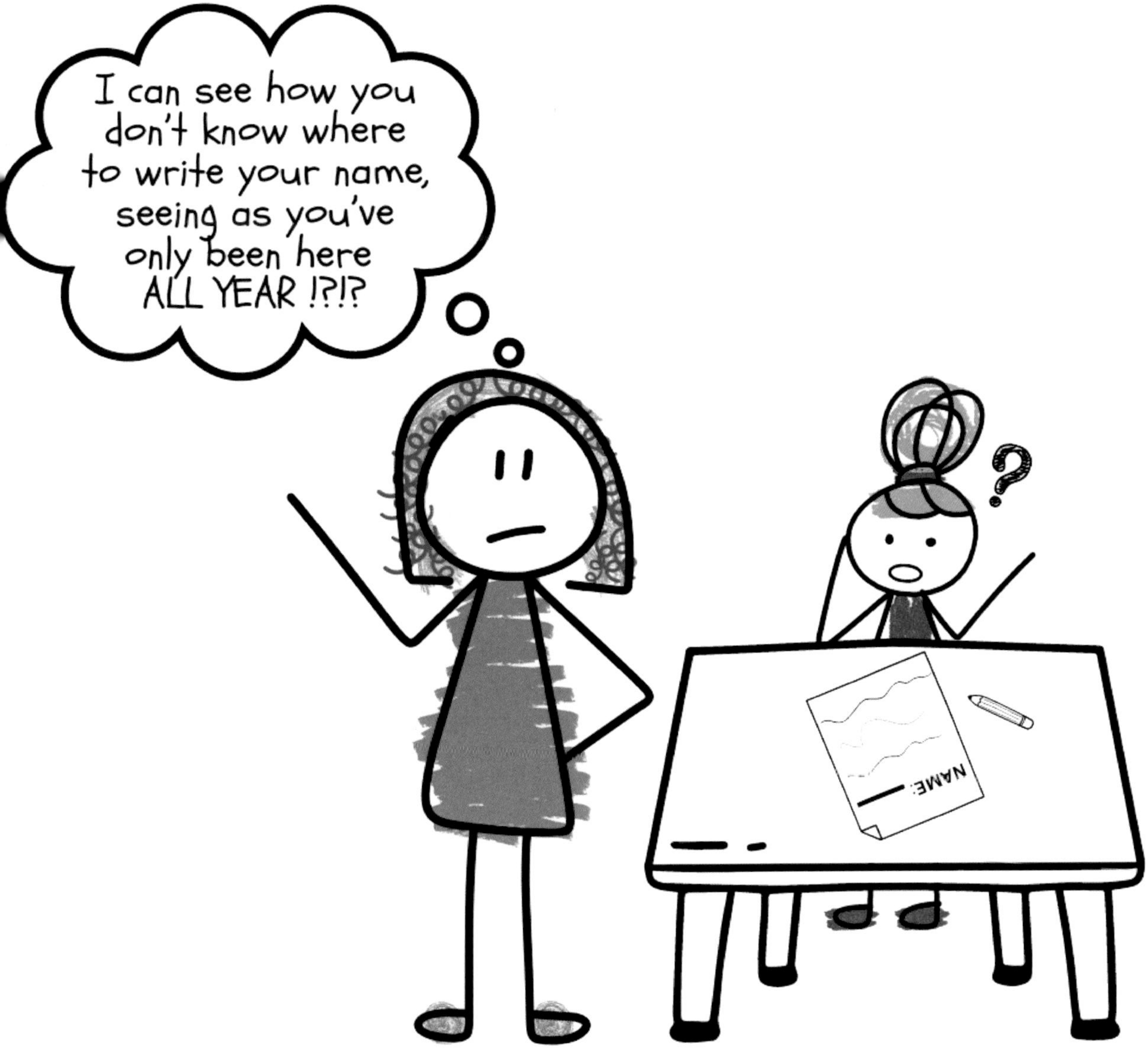
I can see how you don't know where to write your name, seeing as you've only been here ALL YEAR !?!?

Nooooo...

She **thought** to herself...

Was it in the entirety of the time she spent drafting a plan for the relief teacher while feeling unwell, wondering if it would actually take longer to write than the amount of time she was wanting to take off?

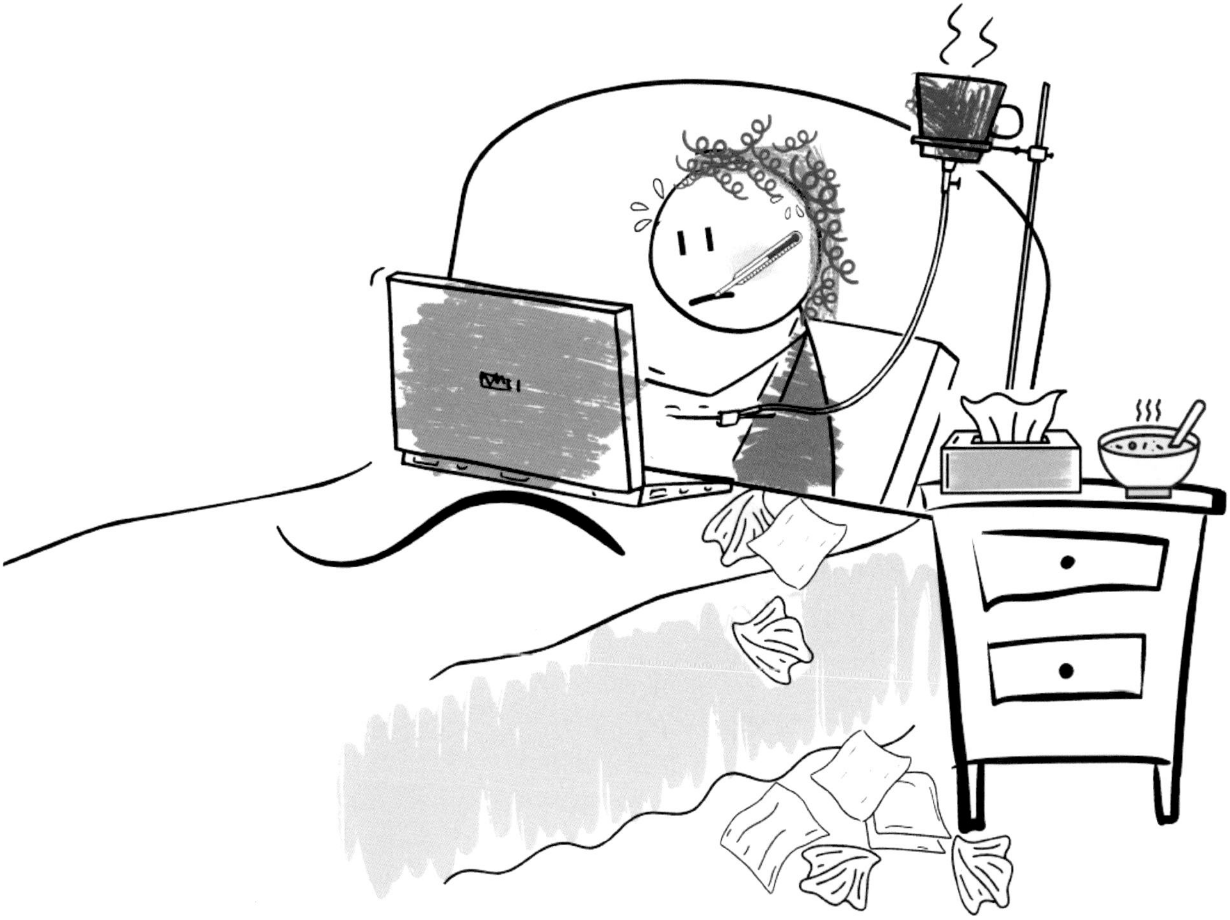

Noooooo...

She **thought** to herself...

Was it in the expression of the parent who appeared for a 'quick 5-minute' visit just as the bell chimed, signaling the start of the class?

This was the very same parent who disregarded her request that parents make an appointment? The same parent who came to inform her, rather impolitely, that it was the teacher's fault that their child hadn't completed his/her homework.

AND, the parent who requested that their child be placed at a different reading level because of their aversion to mundane tasks, questioning why she hadn't engaged with the child more.

AND they blamed the teacher for the missing lunch box, demanding a replacement **AND, AND, AND.**

Noooooo...

She **thought** to herself...

Surely, her smile wasn't at the bottom of the wine glass she poured at the end of a challenging day filled with teaching, marking, managing behaviour, diversifying instruction, attending unpaid mandatory training sessions, participating in whole school, sector, and year-level meetings, engaging in curriculum discussions, filing incident reports, uploading data, meeting with parents, moderating, sick bay notes, dealing with after lunch storytellers, planning lessons, providing first aid, counselling students, and nurturing their growth.

Not to mention the exhaustion accumulated from the multitude of decisions she had made throughout the day, the previous night, and the entire week before.

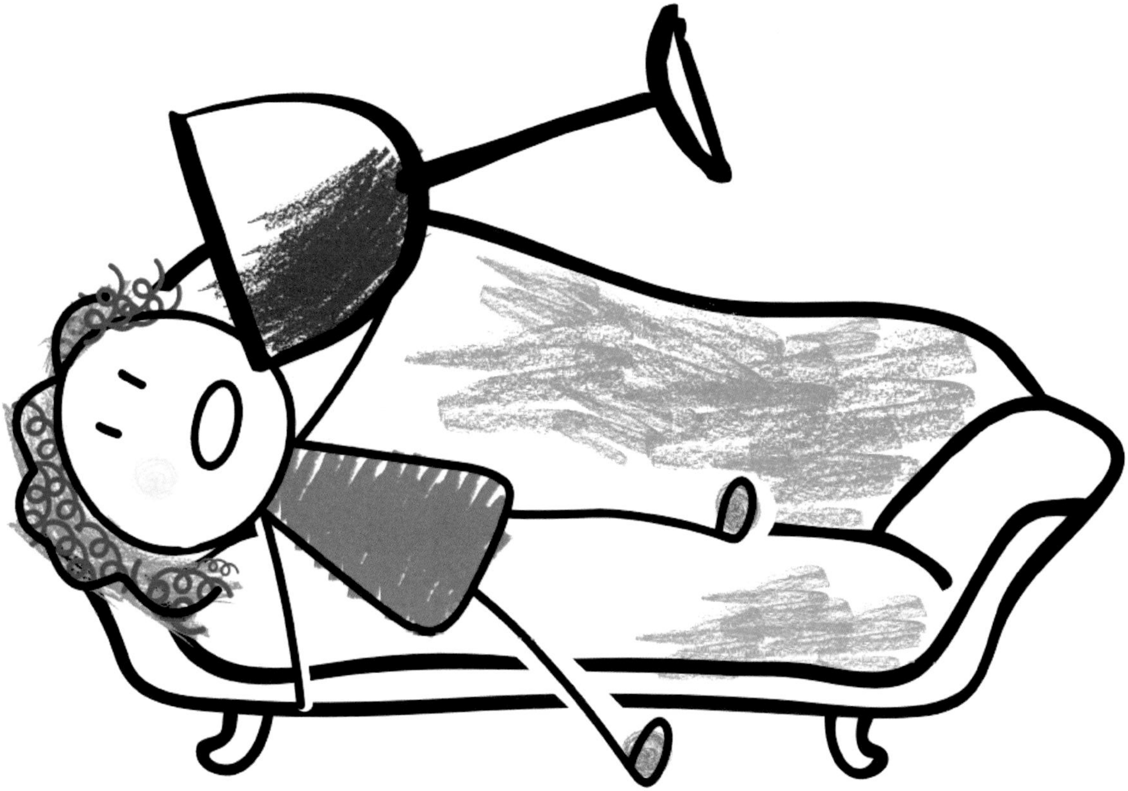

Noooooo...

And just when she thought she'd lost it forever,
there it was, in the faces of all her students who admire
her, look up to her, hang onto her every word,
and cherish her presence.

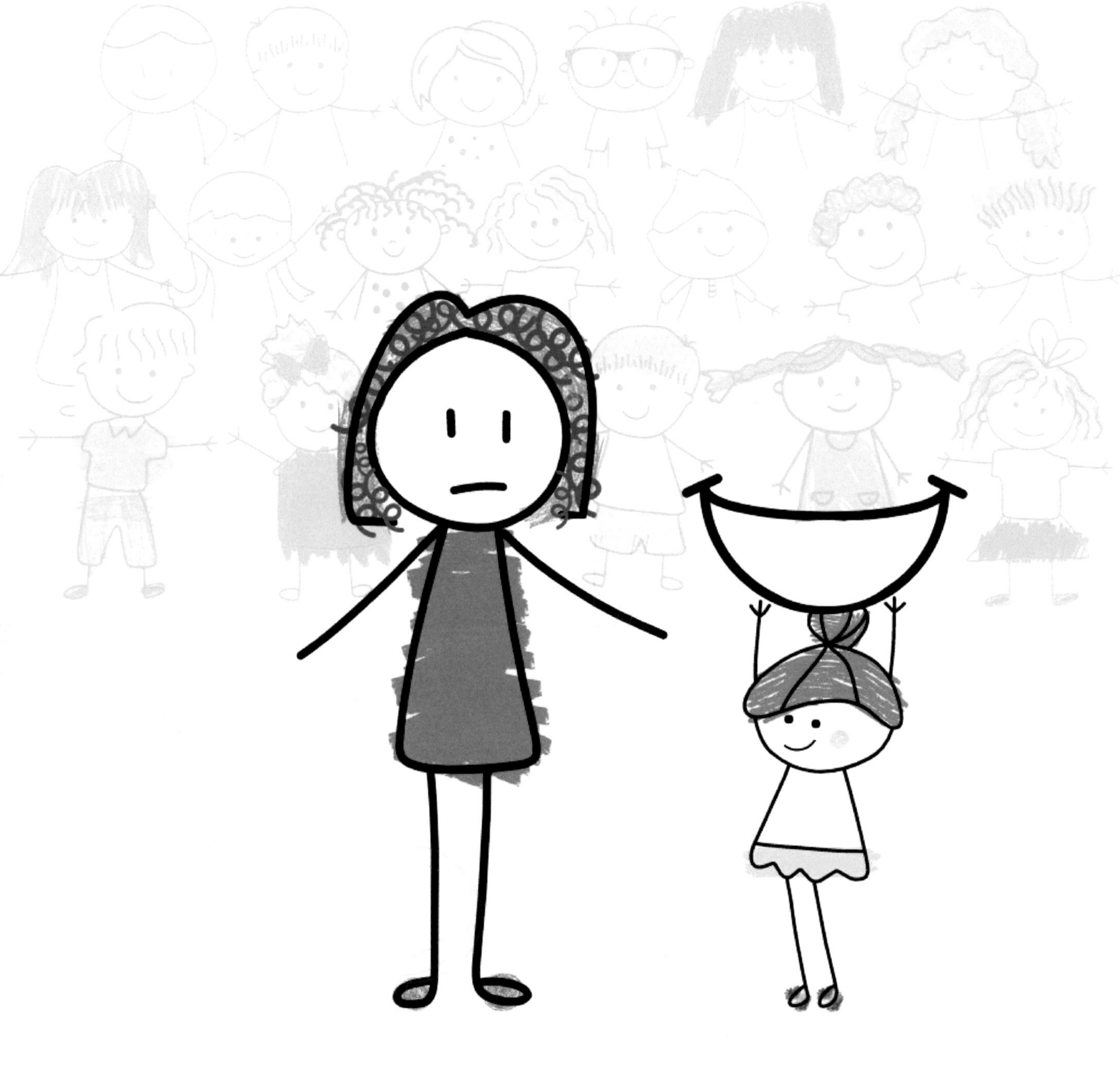

Yesssss!!!

To all the teachers who put tireless effort into each and every student... you are truly and deeply appreciated.
Bec

"I've learned that people will forget what you said,
people will forget what you did,
but people will never forget how you made them feel."

- Maya Angelou -

Why we do what we do...

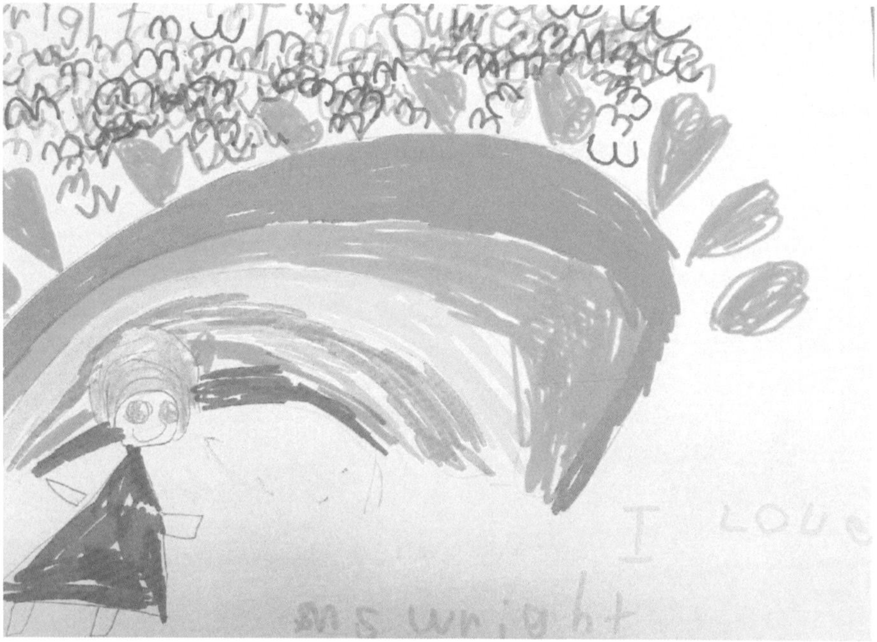
I Love
ms wright

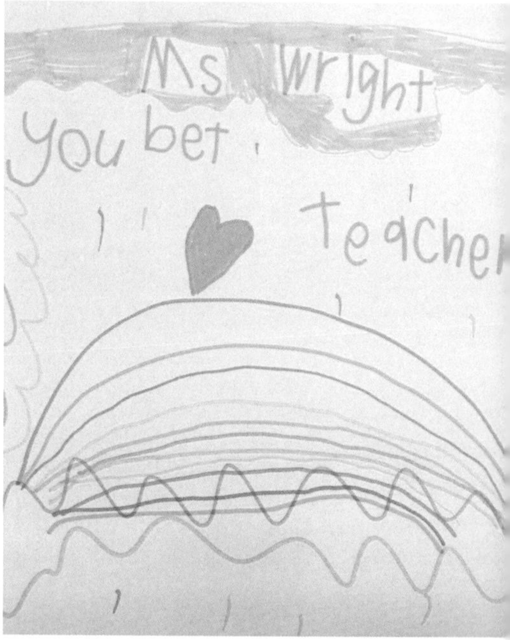
Ms wright
You bet

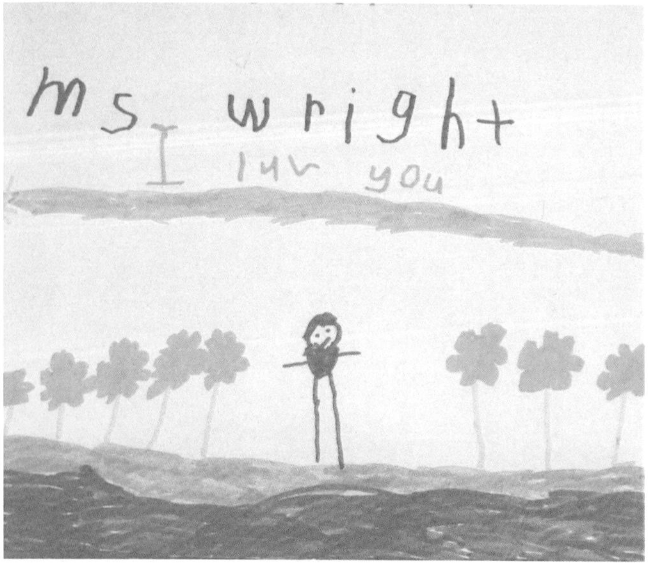
ms wright
I luv you

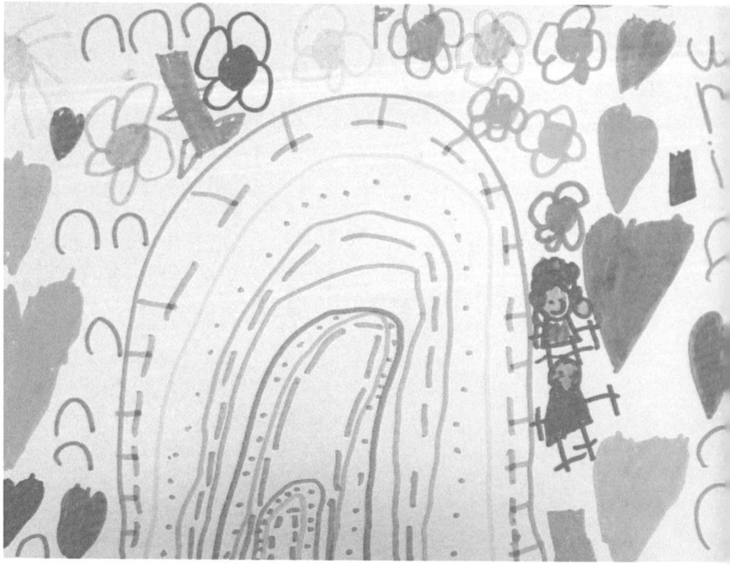

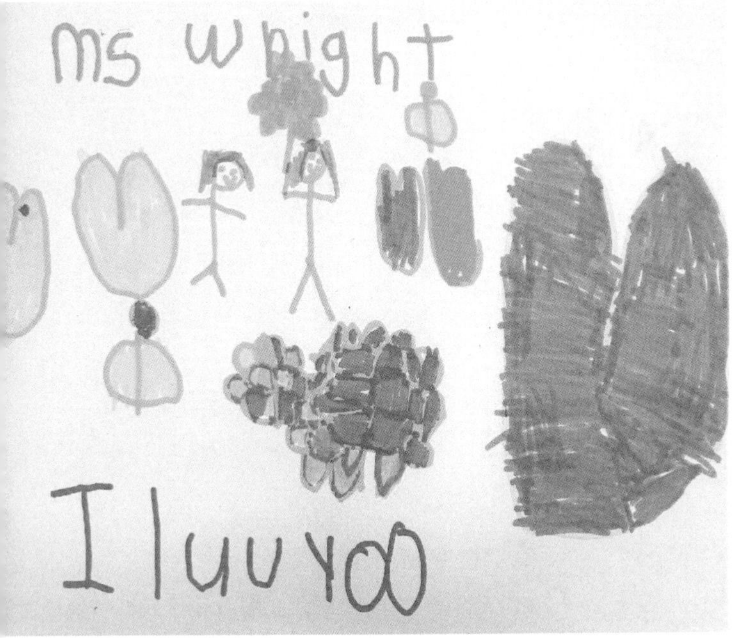
ms wright
I luu Yoo

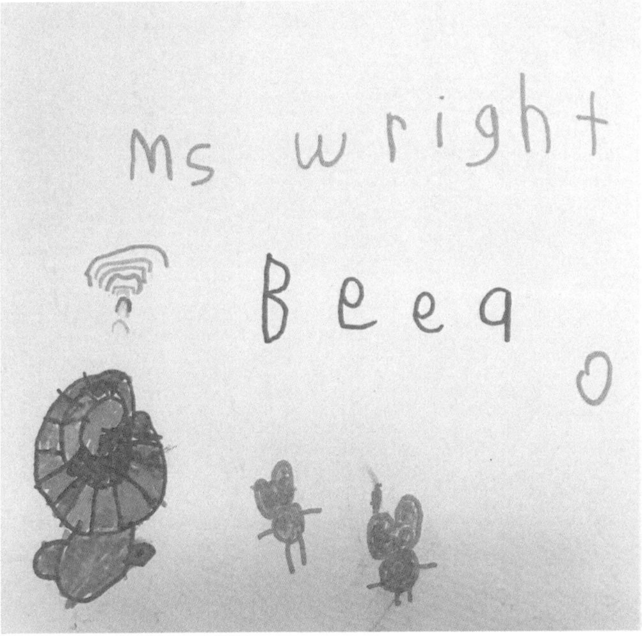
Ms wright
Beeq

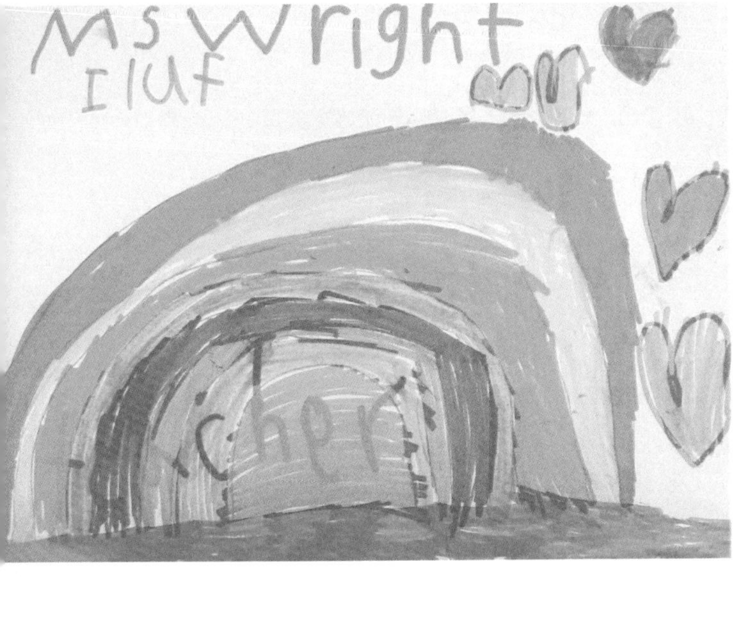
MsWright
ILuf

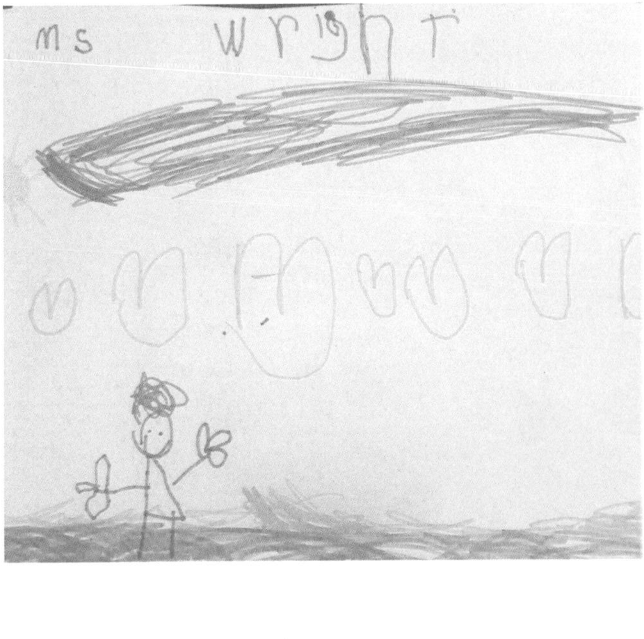
ms wright

About the Author

In the heart of tropical North Queensland, author Bec Wright dedicates her days to educating primary school students, specializing in those with additional needs for over three decades.

A mother to two grown sons, both happily married with children of their own, she finds profound joy in her newfound role as a grandmother.

Following a life-altering car accident, Bec emerged with a newfound appreciation for the vitality of every moment. When not relishing in her grandmother duties, she embraces life to the fullest — whether strumming the bass guitar in the school band, diving into the water for a swim, performing on stage, dancing, or even African drumming.

Driven by an unwavering determination to pursue her aspirations, Bec sets her sights on achieving a lifelong ambition of writing a children's book. Although this narrative may not align precisely with the dreams she held as a 5-year-old, one can only hope that her journey unfolds into a tapestry of dreams yet to be realized.

To contact Bec email becwright@hotmail.com

From the Publisher

In 'The Teacher Who Lost Her Smile,' Bec Wright takes readers on a whimsical journey through the challenges faced by educators. Through a heartfelt narrative, Bec skillfully delves into the universal struggles experienced by teachers everywhere.

The story follows a teacher who, amidst her daily responsibilities, grapples with the loss of her smile. Bec's storytelling prowess shines as she explores the myriad of situations that contribute to the teacher's internal struggle. From the burdens of marking report cards to navigating the complexities of parent-teacher interactions, each predicament resonates with authenticity and poignancy.

What sets this book apart is Bec's ability to infuse humour and warmth into the narrative, despite the weighty subject matter. Moreover, the book's conclusion offers a heartwarming reminder of the profound impact teachers have on their students' lives.

The illustrations, crafted in collaboration with Bec, complement her storytelling beautifully, capturing the essence of each scene with honest charm.

In summary, 'The Teacher Who Lost Her Smile' is a delightful read that celebrates the dedication and resilience of educators. It is a testament to the profound connections forged in the classroom and the enduring power of a teacher's smile.

I would like to wish Bec all the success and joy surrounding the publication of her debut title, 'The Teacher Who Lost Her Smile.' Thank you for shining a light on the unsung heroes in our children's lives, and gifting me the great honour of being your publisher.

Crystal Leonardi
Bowerbird Publishing
www.crystalleonardi.com